REBEL GIRLS BUILD THE FUTURE

In Collaboration with ∞ Meta

18 EXCITING TALES FROM THE METAVERSE

Foreword by Rachel Cross

This is a work of creative nonfiction. It is a collection of heartwarming and thought-provoking stories inspired by the lives of 18 innovators at Meta. It is not an encyclopedic account of the events and accomplishments of their lives.

www.rebelgirls.com

Rebel Girls, Inc.
421 Elm Ave.
Larkspur, CA 94939

Text: Alexis Stratton, Jess Harriton, Sarah Parvis, Shelbi Polk, Sydnee Monday
Art direction: Giulia Flamini
Cover illustrations: xMx.Luo, Thumy Phan, Noa Denmon
Graphic design: Kristen Brittain
Editor: Eliza Kirby
Special thanks: Amy Pfister, Hannah Bennett, Jes Wolfe, Michon Vanderpoel

Printed in China, 2024
10 9 8 7 6 5 4 3 2 1
001-344258-Nov'24
ISBN: 979-8-88964-154-4

CONTENTS

FOREWORD

Dear Rebels,

Growing up, art was my world. I was never far from my colored pencils and sketchbook. I drew my own dresses and dreamed of designing my own house. I immersed myself in digital worlds, from animated movies to interactive video games. I made handcrafted models using everyday materials, and I found any excuse to have my parents take me to the art supply store.

One day, my tech-savvy dad brought home a laser disc player. Laser discs were like DVDs that were the size of vinyl records, and we would spend hours watching behind-the-scenes footage of the special effects in the movies. I was blown away. These artists were like magicians! They used their art to create incredible worlds and transported the audience through time—from a land filled with dinosaurs to a futuristic city with flying cars—and I wanted to be part of that.

The suburb where I lived outside of Toronto, Canada, wasn't exactly known for making movies. And when I asked about classes that combined art and technology, my guidance counselor said they didn't exist! But I was determined to find a way to pursue my passions.

First, I found a web design studio in Toronto. I called them up and convinced them to take me on as their first-ever unpaid intern. A few days a week, I sat next to digital artists and learned how to create online activity pages for kids using a computer program called Photoshop. To make them more fun, I added a cat wearing a pirate outfit or dressed as a medieval knight.

Then I found a school that offered a digital animation course, landed another internship, and eventually worked as a 3D artist on TV shows and music videos. When the opportunity came to work on a movie in Los Angeles, I jumped at it. I headed to California to create special effects and digital sets. And I never looked back. Films, TV, and video games—I have worked on them all.

Today, I get to apply everything I learned about making movies and video games to my work at Meta, a company that helps billions of people around the world connect through apps like Facebook and Instagram. Meta also develops new technologies that make it possible for users to visit the metaverse, a virtual space where people—represented as avatars—can learn, play games, explore, and make friends.

When I discovered my love for art and technology, I was told there wasn't a path for someone with my interests, so I used my curiosity and determination to find my own path. Just like me, Jasmine Bulin and Kate Williams had a passion for art and tech and found creative careers they never knew existed. And Danielle An was also inspired by special effects in movies. She combined her math skills and creativity to become a software engineer. Jenny H. Li found her magic when she taught herself to code and built her own website. Now she works to connect people to the best experiences in the metaverse.

It takes many different roles at Meta to make the metaverse an enjoyable place for everyone—the possibilities are endless! Eleanor Thibeaux's passion for sound and technology led her to become an audio producer. Jahmeilah Roberson helps create worlds where people can play games. Megan Walker uses her graphic design skills to create cool looks and to style animated characters' hair. As you turn these pages, I hope you will be inspired by all the different jobs it takes to build the future.

Dearest Rebel, to find the things you love, be open to learning and trying new things. You may be surprised to discover your passions can lead you to opportunities you've never imagined. Don't be afraid to create your own journey—just because something hasn't been done before doesn't mean it can't be done.

Much love,

Rachel Cross

Rachel Cross, fellow Rebel and head of art for Reality Labs at Meta

BONUS! AUDIO STORIES!

Download the Rebel Girls app and subscribe to listen to hundreds of stories about trailblazing women and girls. Scan here and you'll unlock extended stories of four other innovative women from Meta.

SCAN TO HEAR MORE!

CAROL YIP

STRATEGY AND OPERATIONS LEAD

Once upon a time, a girl named Carol picked up a video camera. She was going to make a movie for her big sister's birthday. Carol wrote a script and then filmed the movie scene by scene. But the best part was when she showed the movie to her sister. *I love making things!* Carol realized. *I love creating experiences.*

Carol never stopped creating. After college, she decided she wanted to be a fashion designer. She even used her own money to start a fashion brand with her best friend. Just like when she made the movie for her sister, Carol poured herself into the project. But something was wrong. She didn't have time to do anything else. She felt herself burning out.

I'm going to be brave, Carol told herself. *I'm going to change my plan*. She knew she wanted to work on something *really* new. She joined Meta (the company that owns Facebook, Instagram, WhatsApp, and other platforms). Right away, she decided it was the place for her. The metaverse is made up of digital spaces where people can come together to share lifelike experiences online. It is a beautiful, colorful, wild world where anything is possible. People can practice using a scalpel without ever setting foot in an operating room. They can sword-fight with an octopus, or step inside an animated movie.

Carol loves working to build the metaverse. Some days, she does simple things like planning topics to talk about in a meeting. Other days, she does complicated things like helping decide what Meta wants to do in the next five years. She's not using a video camera anymore. But she's still making and creating, just like she always wanted to do.

UNITED STATES

"SOMETIMES I FEEL LIKE I HAVE NO IDEA WHAT I'M DOING, BUT IN SOME WAYS, THAT'S WHAT MAKES IT EXCITING."
—CAROL YIP

ILLUSTRATION BY SALINI PERERA

CASSANDRA LEWIS

AVATAR PRODUCT LEAD

Cassandra grew up in Maryland, surrounded by a big family. One day, she sat at a computer with just one other person: her mother. Her mom showed her this amazing system called the Internet. Cassandra could go online and play games and search for things she was interested in, her mom explained.

From there, Cassandra was hooked. She started playing video games and exploring the online world. She was fascinated by science, technology, and building. And she loved imagining what people could do with tech, just like on her favorite TV show, *Star Trek*.

What could this do? She would ask herself each time she encountered a new kind of technology. *What if I took this apart? What if I put it back together in a different way?*

Cassandra went to work for some of the world's biggest tech companies, like Microsoft, Yahoo, and Amazon. She worked on iPads, gaming systems, social media platforms, and e-readers like the Kindle. She kept asking herself the same questions she had asked as a young girl. She kept building, too, and even learned 3D printing. Eventually, she collected six different kinds of printers!

When Cassandra went to work at Meta as a **product lead**, she started building avatars, the icons that represent people in the metaverse. She figures out how people can make the best digital representation of themselves and creates experiences for those avatars. Her computer adventures began with just one other person. And now, in everything she does in the metaverse, Cassandra makes opportunities for many people to connect with one another, no matter where they live.

UNITED STATES AND UNITED KINGDOM

Style

Color

Base Color

ILLUSTRATION BY
NOA DENMON

Highlights

Soft

Dark

"IT'S BEEN
REALLY FUN TO
BRIDGE THE GAP
BETWEEN THE
TECHNICAL AND
CREATIVE."
—CASSANDRA LEWIS

Save

CHELSEA WHITMORE

3D ARTIST

Once upon a time, there was a lonely, imaginative kid who yearned to belong. Their name was Chelsea.

Chelsea loved sharing homemade potstickers with their mom and having deep philosophical conversations with their dad. But they had a hard time making friends. Then one day, a new student showed up at their school in California. She looked lonely too. Gathering all their courage, Chelsea walked up to her and whispered, "Do you like Neopets?"

Neopets was an online game where players could adopt and take care of virtual pets—feeding them, buying them toys, and playing with them.

To Chelsea's relief, the new girl said, "Yes!"

The two became fast friends. They chatted together, played together, and made up stories together.

Along with Neopets and other video games, Chelsea loved reading, drawing, and inventing new characters and fantastical worlds. So, when Chelsea got older, they decided to build worlds and experiences that made an impact on people and helped them connect—just like others had built for them. They studied game art in college, learning skills like how to make environments change rapidly so players felt like they were moving, and how to use digital tools to sculpt characters as if they were working with clay.

Today, as a **3D artist** for the metaverse, Chelsea does a lot of different jobs—sometimes they help create games, sometimes they make rewards for quests, and sometimes they design **prototypes** of new features.

In many ways, the metaverse reminds Chelsea of Neopets: Chelsea and their team create a digital universe where players get to make their own worlds, full of meaning, stories, connection—and pets!

 UNITED STATES

"THE METAVERSE CONNECTS PEOPLE—PEOPLE MAKE FRIENDSHIPS HERE! IN A SOMETIMES LONELY, SOMETIMES ISOLATING WORLD, THAT'S POWERFUL."
—CHELSEA WHITMORE

ILLUSTRATION BY THUMY PHAN

DANIELLE AN

SOFTWARE ENGINEER

Danielle started learning math before she was old enough to talk. Geometry always intrigued her. She loved the elegance of triangles, parallel lines, and 3D shapes. She didn't spend much time making art, but she did feel a creative spark inside her. Her mother expressed herself with funky, stylish clothes, and Danielle looked up to her. *What would it be like to be a fashion designer?* she wondered.

Watching *The Lord of the Rings: The Return of the King* as a teenager changed Danielle's life. The movie was the third in a series. She hadn't seen the first two movies and didn't know the story. But the special effects captivated her. The sweeping landscapes of Middle-earth, the glowing beauty of an elf queen, and the ghostly motions of ancient warriors were out of this world. Sitting in the theater, she knew she wanted to work on films like this one.

Danielle decided to study computer graphics, which put her excellent math skills to use. She went on to work on film series like *How to Train Your Dragon, Shrek,* and *Toy Story.* And then her interests led her to the technology industry.

Today, Danielle is helping to reinvent fashion in the metaverse as a **software architect**. She asks big questions about what it means to wear outfits in **virtual reality** worlds. What if you could put on a dress made of bubbles that turn colors when you're happy? What if you could wear a business suit for a meeting, then instantly change into a fire dress for a night out? Danielle still uses her math and logic skills, but she also gets to express the creativity she has felt inside since she was young.

CHINA AND UNITED STATES

ILLUSTRATION BY
JIAWEN CHEN

ELEANOR THIBEAUX

AUDIO PRODUCER

Growing up in Spring, Texas, whenever Eleanor saw something that wasn't right, she would speak up. One day, when she and her friends were playing an imagining game, they saw a girl hiding from some bullies. Right away, Eleanor asked her to play. That girl, Meaghan, became Eleanor's best friend, and her ideas made the storytelling games even better.

Stories and music filled Eleanor's home. Her mother sang in a choir, and she and her brothers took voice and piano lessons. Eleanor loved to perform along with musical soundtracks. With *Oliver & Company* on her TV, she'd sing along with the orphaned kitty, puppy pickpockets, and grumpy street vendors.

As she grew older, Eleanor found a new interest: the Internet. She spent hours with Meaghan and their other friends playing games online. The Internet was a way to dive deep into stories and connect with other people.

In college, Eleanor explored the world of sound technology. After getting a degree in **audio engineering**, Eleanor realized that she could combine her love of storytelling and her love of sound into what she calls a *super passion.* As an **audio producer**, she could use all kinds of sounds, including music, to make experiences come alive for audiences.

Eleanor started working as an audio producer at Meta, where she's in charge of thinking about how sound can help make people feel like they are in a different place or a different time. Eleanor knows that the people who use the metaverse have all sorts of interests and abilities, and she wants them all to feel welcome. What about someone who is blind? What about someone with limited **mobility**? Just like on that long-ago day when she invited her future best friend to play, Eleanor is determined to include everyone.

"YOU ARE ALREADY EVERY SINGLE THING YOU NEED TO BE IN ORDER TO SUCCEED."
—ELEANOR THIBEAUX

ILLUSTRATION BY
HANNAH AGOSTA

GINGER LARSEN

GAME PRODUCER

One day when Ginger was in fifth grade, someone gave her teacher a big box of costumes. Ginger leaped from her chair and grabbed a gorgeous frilly dress from the box. She put it on right then and there. Then she swished out the door, pretending she was a fancy lady, and strolled out into the sun, fully embodying the character she had created.

Hey, what's Ginger doing outside? a classmate asked as Ginger moseyed past the window. *Should someone get her?* another piped up.

Ginger marches to the beat of her own drum, her teacher said. *She'll come back when she's ready.* And sure enough, she did.

Ginger kept making up stories for herself. A lot of the time, they involved animals, who seemed like furry little people to her. Ginger's dad was a tech fan and always made sure she had the newest cool video games. She tried out game after game, but when she discovered *Animal Planet: The Ultimate Wildlife Adventure!*, she fell in love. Through the screen, she could explore habitats and learn about all kinds of creatures.

When Ginger started working as a **game producer** for Meta, she couldn't believe she got paid to make and play games. She uses her imagination to help other people enjoy imaginary places. Her job is to make sure **virtual reality** and other games are fun to play and easy to learn—and that they look awesome.

Ginger says, "I follow the path that feels right to me, letting my internal compass guide me regardless of what others think or say." Thanks to her work, people in the metaverse can do the same: they can be whoever they want to be.

UNITED STATES

"THERE ARE NO PRE-ESTABLISHED RULES OR NORMS FOR WHAT WE ARE BUILDING, SO IT REQUIRES A LOT OF CREATIVITY TO OVERCOME THE OBSTACLES INVOLVED." —GINGER LARSEN

ILLUSTRATION BY SOFIE BIRKIN

HAI-NHU TRAN

CONTENT DESIGN DIRECTOR

There once was a baby named Hai-Nhu who spent five days crossing the ocean in a tippy homemade boat. She and her family were refugees from Vietnam, and they were running out of food and water. Hai-Nhu and her family were rescued and found their way to San Francisco. They were so happy to be safe.

Hai-Nhu lived with her mom, her brother, and five other relatives in a tiny apartment. Her dad had to stay back in Vietnam. Her family didn't have much money, but they supported one another as best they could. They often shared their joy over family dinners. They'd talk and laugh as they ate delicious dishes prepared with care by Hai-Nhu's mom and aunts. The family bonded over sizzling fish, crisp bean sprouts, and crunchy spring rolls.

A practical job is what you need, Hai-Nhu's family told her. She agreed. *I'll study chemistry in college*, she thought. *That's practical*. But after two years, Hai-Nhu had a terrible feeling that she had made the wrong choice. She didn't even *like* chemistry! So she switched to studying English instead. Her family did *not* think this was a good move. *How will you get a job?* they asked her.

Hai-Nhu didn't know. But she did know she liked writing. Maybe she'd become a technical writer. Hai-Nhu took a writing job at a tech company. Soon she realized that while she was good at writing, she was great at leading other people.

When Hai-Nhu became a director of **content design** at Meta, she knew she had found the right fit. She loved helping her team, answering their questions, and making suggestions. Hai-Nhu says, "I work at the intersection of language and leadership, which are two things I never expected to have in a career. I ended up finding my passions, after all."

VIETNAM AND UNITED STATES

"I'M INSPIRED TO DESIGN EXPERIENCES WHERE PEOPLE CAN BRING THEIR AUTHENTIC SELVES AND MAKE MEANINGFUL CONNECTIONS WITH OTHERS."
—HAI-NHU TRAN

ILLUSTRATION BY THUMY PHAN

JAHMEILAH ROBERSON

PRODUCT DESIGNER

As a child, Jahmeilah spent her days exploring, playing sports, and making up games with the other kids in her neighborhood. With her vivid imagination, she was always dreaming up new adventures. She'd stay outdoors all day until the streetlights came on. When she did spend time inside, she loved playing video games and trying out the new technology her parents brought home from their jobs in **Silicon Valley**.

In college, she stayed busy, pursuing her love of sports. But as the only person of color on the volleyball team, she struggled to find a sense of belonging. She left the team and explored the other amazing things her school had to offer, finding joy and community in the Alpha Kappa Alpha sorority, which was founded by Black college students more than 100 years ago. She also discovered a passion for design and research within the world of computer science.

After graduation, Jahmeilah traveled the world doing research. But she wanted to see and feel the impact of her work. So, back to the world of gaming she went. She was amazed to see how many different people—from writers to musicians to business people—worked together to bring a game to life.

Ever since adventuring with her neighbors as a kid, Jahmeilah has been great at connecting with others. And now, she gets to help people connect across the metaverse. She's a **product designer**, which means she helps create **virtual reality** worlds where people can play games, create, and interact. "We are building the future of interaction and changing the way people engage with each other," she says. Thanks to designers like Jahmeilah, anyone can go on adventures together, whether they live in the same neighborhood or on opposite sides of the world.

UNITED STATES

ILLUSTRATION BY
NOA DENMON

"WITH SO MANY
DIFFERENT TALENTS
NEEDED TO CREATE
GREAT PRODUCTS,
THERE'S ROOM
AT THE TABLE FOR
EVERY BACKGROUND
AND FIELD."
—JAHMEILAH ROBERSON

JASMINE BULIN

GAME DESIGNER

Growing up, Jasmine was always making something. Sometimes she wrote poetry and drew colorful illustrations. Other times she devised science experiments, creating exploding volcanoes or mixing strange elixirs. Then there were the days when she used screwdrivers and pliers to take machines apart just to see how they worked. She *usually* managed to put them back together . . .

When people asked her what she wanted to be when she grew up, she often said, "An artist!" But she also said, "A scientist!" Because, really, she wanted to be *both*. Art and science seemed so far apart she couldn't imagine a job where the two fields overlapped.

In college, she studied both art and computer science. Then she discovered a job she didn't even know existed: game designer. She soon realized it was a role that brought together art and science—as well as all her creativity, curiosity, and love of technology.

As a game designer, Jasmine worked with teams of other makers to create games and apps that were fun, educational, and even useful in the real world. One game she designed helped an actual mission to the moon. Another taught players how to negotiate and solve problems.

Today, she works on the metaverse, building a massive virtual world where people from across the globe can be creative together.

Jasmine loves creating virtual spaces where players can learn, explore, and make friends. And as the metaverse grows, she can't wait to see the new stories people dream up, the inventions they create, and the collaborations that make those dreams possible.

UNITED STATES

"EVERY GAME DESIGN BEGINS WITH THE SPARK OF CREATIVITY, FOLLOWED BY ALL THE WORK TO MAKE IT REAL."
—JASMINE BULIN

ILLUSTRATION BY HANNAH AGOSTA

JENNY H. LI

PRODUCT MANAGER

Jenny was 25th chair when she started orchestra at her high school in Ann Arbor, Michigan. In orchestras, players who sit in the first chairs are considered the best. Jenny knew she was good, and she was determined to rise to the top.

So, she challenged the 24th chair. In a challenge, both players perform the same music, and the conductor decides who played best. The winner gets the higher chair.

Jenny beat the 24th chair—and the 23rd, and the 22nd. In a *single day,* she went from 25th chair all the way to second. In that moment, she knew that hard work and perseverance could change her world.

She carried that lesson with her into the future. It was especially helpful when she decided to change careers. After earning her business degree, Jenny worked in finance, but she always remembered playing on computers as a kid. Once, she'd found one of her dad's computer books and used it to code her own webpage. When the page lit up on the computer screen, it felt like magic!

After years of working in business, Jenny wanted to feel that magic again. But she couldn't find a tech company that wanted to hire someone with a passion for tech but no experience.

Each job application was met with rejection. But just like in high school, Jenny didn't give up. Many applications later, a **startup** company took a chance on her, and eventually, she joined the team at Meta. Today, she's a product manager who works with engineers, designers, and **marketers** to connect users to the best experiences for them in the metaverse.

Working in the metaverse is like a dream come true for Jenny—even better than winning first chair. And it still feels pretty magical.

CHINA AND UNITED STATES

product road map

"NO MATTER WHAT
TITLE YOU HAVE OR
FIELD YOU'RE IN,
EVERYTHING IS
ABOUT SOLVING
IMPORTANT
PROBLEMS."
—JENNY H. LI

ILLUSTRATION BY
XMX.LUO

KATE WILLIAMS

At three years old, Kate got some news that made her feel different. She was diagnosed with type 1 diabetes. It meant that her body didn't make enough insulin, a substance that turns the sugar in food into energy. She would need to take medication for the rest of her life.

Sometimes it felt like she had to fight hard to do the same things other kids did. But she learned that she *could* do them—it just took some extra work.

Kate always had a creative streak. As a little girl, she loved putting on shows for her family. She would sing and dance and play silly characters with her sister and her cousins. She liked it best when she was the director *and* the star!

As she got older, Kate knew she wanted to do something creative in tech. She didn't know what though. So she learned all about art and design and how to use them in the world of technology. But instead of making art all day, she always found herself helping others manage their projects. As problems popped up—and they always did—Kate was there to help her team find clever ways forward.

This kind of work really is creative, she realized.

She knew she would make mistakes. And she says she still does, almost every day. But she also knows that mistakes are how she and her colleagues learn. The metaverse is brand-new, so they're inventing the world as they work—with resilience and creativity. And those are two things Kate knows she's good at. After all, she has been practicing them ever since she was a little girl.

UNITED STATES

"THIS TECHNOLOGY IS CHANGING THE WORLD, AND WE ARE SHAPING IT. IT'S INCREDIBLE."
—KATE WILLIAMS

ILLUSTRATION BY SOFIE BIRKIN

MEAGHAN FITZGERALD

PRODUCT MARKETER

When Meaghan was three years old, she lined up her stuffed animals every morning. *Don't forget to do your chores today!* she'd tell them. *Does everyone have what they need?* Her parents called her the "CEO of the bedroom" because she took care of everyone—and kept them on task too!

As Meaghan grew, so did her imagination. She created a pretend detective agency, searched for rare jewels among rocks, and built entire societies out of LEGO bricks. When she got old enough to use the family's computer, she started making posters and digital artwork. She was amazed at the many ways she could express her creativity through technology.

Today, Meaghan's career as a product **marketer** combines her creativity and her love of technology. She asks lots of people about their ideas for the metaverse and helps engineers bring those ideas to life. Then when a new feature is ready, she tells the world about it. She's also the boss of more than 25 people across the United States and the United Kingdom. She makes sure everyone has what they need, just like she used to do for the stuffed animals in her bedroom.

Meaghan is excited to help expand everything people can do in the metaverse. Her family lives far away—some all the way in South Africa—but they can spend time together in the metaverse without leaving their living rooms. "I love that we can all pop on a **VR headset** and feel like we are going on a trip, playing a game, or watching a movie together, and I can't wait for it to get even easier and better," she says.

"I LOVE BEING THE FIRST TO TRY NEW THINGS AND THEN SHARE THEM WITH PEOPLE ALL OVER THE WORLD."
—MEAGHAN FITZGERALD

ILLUSTRATION BY ESTHER LALANNE

MEGAN WALKER

LOOK DEVELOPMENT ARTIST

As soon as Megan could hold a pencil, she began searching for something artistic to do. Later, she would pair hand-drawn pictures with swirly letters to make greeting cards for her friends. In her small Texas country town, there wasn't a lot of art around, but that didn't stop her from exploring and trying new things. When she wasn't making art, she was playing video games with her brother. Her favorite game was *Final Fantasy IV*, and her favorite character was Rydia. Rydia was magical and powerful—and she had amazing hair. *How do they get her hair to look like that?* Megan sometimes wondered, watching Rydia's bright-green tresses move as she ran and jumped.

When Megan discovered graphic design in high school, she knew she had found a way to combine her two passions. She could use computers to create art! She went to college to study graphic design, and after she graduated, she went to work at DreamWorks Animation, creating looks for different animated characters. She became an artist, then a boss of other artists. As she worked on movies, she became an expert on styling animated characters' hair. Short spiky pixie cuts, long looping braids, wild curly manes—she could create them all. She even developed a new tool that artists could use to groom their characters' hair.

Megan took her new skills with her to Meta, where she began designing the hair and other items for avatars. She directed other artists and worked with engineers to find technological ways to bring the artists' visions to life. Megan loves to picture the metaverse as a place where people can have any appearance they want: "Those characters my brother and I would imagine ourselves being could become a reality in the metaverse!"

UNITED STATES

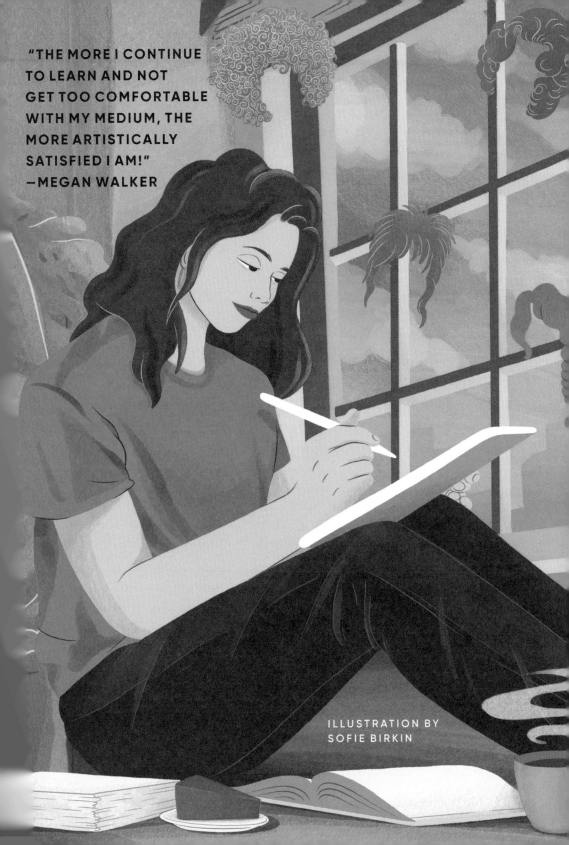

"THE MORE I CONTINUE TO LEARN AND NOT GET TOO COMFORTABLE WITH MY MEDIUM, THE MORE ARTISTICALLY SATISFIED I AM!"
—MEGAN WALKER

ILLUSTRATION BY SOFIE BIRKIN

MING LUO

TECHNICAL ARTIST

Ming remembers the day when she clicked a cartridge into her brother's video game console for the first time. The small black-and-white TV buzzed to life, and the pixelated images sent her on an amazing adventure. From that day on, she couldn't stop thinking about exploring the digital world.

Ming worked hard in school and earned a degree in electronics. When she was 20 years old, she took a huge step—she moved from China to the United States. At her new school in the US, Ming learned about designing video games and creating special effects in animated movies. Best of all, she got to work on an exciting project: designing the vehicle path for a new *Star Wars* ride!

But in 2018, Ming hit a bump in the road. She lost her job. Suddenly, her future was uncertain. She needed a job to keep her visa, which is a government document that allows her to stay and work in the US. She couldn't bear the thought of leaving her partner and friends behind and giving up a career that she loved. For two intense months, Ming dedicated herself to learning new skills. Just before her deadline for returning to China, she landed a job at Meta. Her visa was renewed, and she could stay!

Today, Ming works as a technical artist who specializes in creating extended reality experiences. With extended reality technology, you can wear a headset that lets you wander through an ancient castle, explore the surface of Mars, or jump around a made-up marshmallow world. Or you can use a device to show digital images in the real world. Designers come to her with big ideas, and she uses her technical skills to make them happen in the metaverse. Ming is doing more than exploring the digital world. She's creating it!

CHINA AND UNITED STATES

"IN THIS DIGITAL REALM, WE CAN BE ANYONE OR ANYTHING WE IMAGINE."
—MING LUO

ILLUSTRATION BY
JIAWEN CHEN

NAN LI

LEAD ANIMATOR

Once upon a time, a little girl named Nan grew up in China surrounded by cartoons. She would sit in the glow of the TV, watching her favorite shows. When the episodes ended, she would draw the characters she had seen on the screen. Her favorites were princesses, and she tore through coloring book after coloring book, filling in their flowy dresses and sparkling tiaras. When she was in high school, she read a magazine article about **animators**, the people who make images move and express stories. *That's what I want to do!* Nan thought.

She realized that before she could be an animator, she had to become an artist. So, she began doing art projects outside of school. She studied on her own and did extra lessons at home in the evenings and on weekends. Nan aced both her art and academic exams and went to her dream school to study animation.

For her graduation project, she had to create an animated short film. A movie like this usually has a whole team of people working on it for years. Nan had only one other teammate and six months to pull it off! The pair pushed through and ended up winning awards for their work.

Later, after moving to California, Nan got a job as an animator for a video game company. She worked on *The Sims*. In this game, people invent pretend versions of themselves and their lives. She loved dreaming up new characters in her studio. She imagined their personalities and their stories, whether they were a wizard, a mermaid, or an ordinary person.

Next up, Nan landed her dream job at Meta. Now she animates characters in the metaverse. "In the metaverse," she says, "you have the freedom to embody any identity and engage in limitless activities."

CHINA AND UNITED STATES

"AS ANIMATORS, OUR MISSION IS TO BREATHE SOUL INTO CHARACTERS." —NAN LI

ILLUSTRATION BY XMX.LUO

SACH SACHITHANANDAN

ART DEPARTMENT MANAGER

Once upon a time, on a tea plantation in Sri Lanka, a young girl named Sevvanthie sat nestled among the roots of a giant bamboo plant, staring up at the shivering leaves and dreaming up fantastical stories. Sevvanthie, or Sach as she was later known, loved reading books in the lush green tea fields.

These peaceful moments were her favorites—but they were brief. Throughout Sach's youth, Sri Lankans suffered through a civil war. Sach's home was destroyed in the fighting, and Sach, her parents, and her brother lost everything they had. She was even separated from her mom and dad for a while—going to school in a big city while they rebuilt their lives in a small town. Every day, Sach missed her mom and dad, but they taught her that her education was something that could never be destroyed.

When Sach graduated high school, she was determined to go to college. But all the Sri Lankan universities were closed because of the war.

So, Sach made a brave leap: she moved to the other side of the world. At a university in the United States, Sach studied illustration and animation, making the stories she dreamed up appear on the page. Soon, she was drawing every day, and as she sat before a sketch pad, she realized she had found her true home.

Eventually, Sach's love of stories brought her to 3D art, and she worked in game art for 20 years. Today, as an art department manager for Meta, she helps teams of artists create and evolve the company's avatars. With family scattered across the globe, Sach loves that the metaverse brings people together across space and time. One day, she hopes the metaverse will help everyone connect in ways that feel as "real" as the physical world.

SRI LANKA AND UNITED STATES

"BUILDING THE METAVERSE
FEELS LIKE SAILING AN ARMADA
IN A MULTIDIMENSIONAL SEA."
—SACH SACHITHANANDAN

ILLUSTRATION BY
SALINI PERERA

SARA CINA

DATA SCIENTIST

When Sara was growing up in Philadelphia, her dad bought a computer for their family. *The Internet is here!* Sara thought. She heard the screeches and static buzz of the dial-up modem connection in her home. That was the sound of information going out over the wires in the house. It seemed powerful to Sara—and magical.

Sara loved imagining what technology could do for humans. She liked to read science fiction and watch *Star Trek: The Next Generation* on TV. But even though her favorite TV characters were blasting off to universes far away on their spaceship, the *Enterprise,* Sara decided to stay firmly planted on Earth. In college, she began studying geology.

Learning about the Earth and its rocks, hiking in India and Mongolia, and getting a PhD felt good to Sara. She loved being outside and sharing her expertise with her students. But she missed numbers. When the COVID-19 pandemic came, the world stopped, and Sara took a long, hard look at her life. *What do I really want to do for work?* she asked herself. Some of her friends were working at Meta. They liked it. And there, she could play with data and numbers.

Sara became a data scientist at the company. Now she studies how people use Meta's products, collecting data along the way. Sometimes she designs experiments to see if users would like a product better if something changed. And once she's confident in her findings, she tells the rest of the team what the users thought. In this way, Sara helps make sure the metaverse gets better and better.

The technology she works with is powerful. Will it take humans as far as the starship *Enterprise*? Sara doesn't know. But she's ready to find out.

UNITED STATES AND SWITZERLAND

"THE PROCESS OF LEARNING OFTEN FEELS UNCOMFORTABLE, BECAUSE IT'S DIFFICULT TO PUSH PAST THE BOUNDARY OF WHAT YOU ARE ALREADY GOOD AT. YOU HAVE TO BE BAD AT SOMETHING BEFORE YOU CAN BE GOOD AT IT."
—SARA CINA

ILLUSTRATION BY HANNAH AGOSTA

SARAH COONEY

TECHNICAL ART MANAGER

One lucky day, when Sarah was young, her parents won a Macintosh computer in a contest—and gave it to her. At first, she was more interested in taking the computer apart than learning how to use it. She tapped at the keyboard's keys and gaped as the screen turned on, wondering how it all worked.

As she got older, she played educational games, learned how to type, and made her very first digital drawings. Sarah had long loved painting and drawing, and she stared in wonder as her creations took shape on the screen.

How do these programs work? she asked herself. *Could I make a program like this someday?*

Sarah's passion for computers led her to study software engineering in college. Later, she went back to school to learn about digital and traditional arts.

Since then, she has merged her interests in computers and art, working on projects big and small—from video games and animation to feature films and social apps. Today, she's a tech art manager. She and her teammates create avatars so users can choose how they want to appear in the metaverse. Sarah and her team want to make every look possible in the virtual world. So, together, they design tons of options for avatar faces, hairstyles, makeup, clothing, accessories, movement, expressions, and interactions.

As an artist and an engineer, Sarah loves the blank canvas of the metaverse and all the possibilities it offers. She hopes the metaverse will help break down barriers and build connections "to people, to objects, to spaces, to knowledge, and more."

UNITED STATES

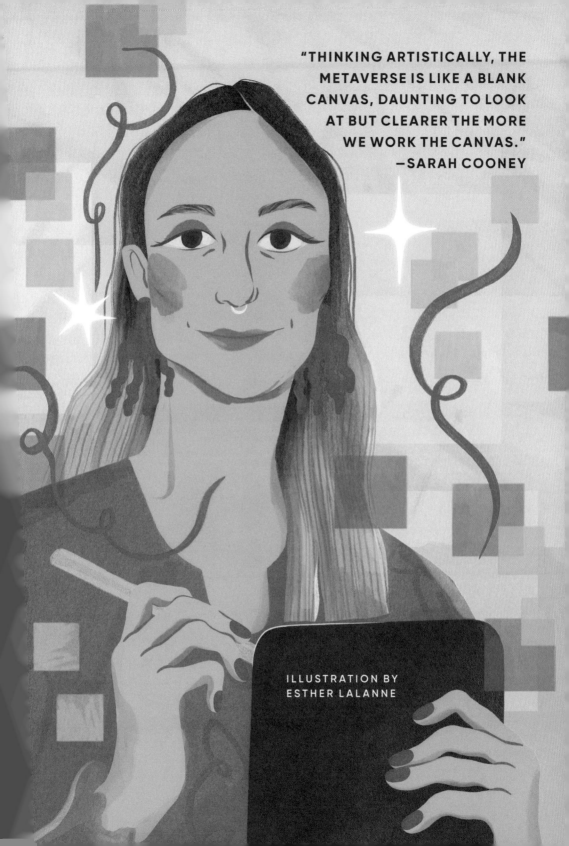

"THINKING ARTISTICALLY, THE METAVERSE IS LIKE A BLANK CANVAS, DAUNTING TO LOOK AT BUT CLEARER THE MORE WE WORK THE CANVAS."
—SARAH COONEY

ILLUSTRATION BY ESTHER LALANNE

TELL YOUR TALE

Write Your Story

It's time to explore the Rebel you know the best—you! All you need is a piece of paper, something to write and draw with, and your imagination. Fold a piece of paper in half, like a booklet, then unfold it.

Think about how you want to tell your story. What would you want readers to know about you if you were featured in a Rebel Girls book? On the left side of the fold, write your name in big, bright letters. Then write your story.

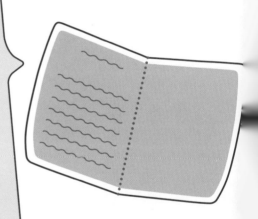

STORYTELLING TIPS

There are lots of ways to tell your story.

- You can start with "Once upon a time . . ." like in Carol Yip's story, or jump right into the action like in Jenny H. Li's.
- Consider telling a story about when you were little or sharing a moment when you were extra proud of yourself.
- Make sure to add lots of details.
- If you are describing a moment in your life, close your eyes and remember what it was like. Then write down what it looked like, how it smelled, and the sounds you heard.

Draw Your Portrait

Channel your inner artist and make a self-portrait.

- Would you like to draw or paint? What materials would you like to use? Colored pencils? Crayons? Pens? Watercolors? Gather your supplies.
- On the right side of the fold, draw your portrait.
- When you're done, you can share your story and portrait with a friend or family member, hang it up, or even keep it tucked inside this book.

UNIQUE YOU

Every self-portrait is different. What do you want your picture to show?

- You can show yourself posing like Sarah Cooney, or doing an activity like Ginger Larsen.
- You can focus on your face, or show yourself from your head to your feet — or anything in between.
- The portrait can be realistic or abstract, colorful or black-and-white — however you see yourself.
- Don't forget the background! It, too, can be either realistic or abstract. What does the background of your portrait reveal about you?

DREAM UP YOUR OWN DIGITAL WORLD

Join forces with Rachel Cross, the head of art for Reality Labs, and come up with your own digital world for the metaverse.

- **Set up your workspace.** Before you dive in, take a moment to organize your space. What do you need to create? Some paper for drawing, sketching, and jotting down ideas? Colored pencils, pens, markers, or crayons for drawing and coloring? A tablet or computer for digital designs? Collect your materials and devices.

   What else do you need to get your creative juices flowing? Fuzzy socks and your favorite tunes? A cup of warm tea and some calming audio soundscapes? Set up your creative space to give your imagination a playground.

- **Design an avatar.** An online avatar is a digital character that represents a particular person. In this case: you! Avatars can be flat, 2D illustrations that work just like profile photos. They can be 3D images. They can also be animated, so you can make them move about in digital worlds.

Do you want your avatar to look just like you—with your hair color, eye color, body shape, and clothing style? Do you want a more fantastical representation? You might choose to look realistic or more like a fairy or a robot.

Think about what you want your avatar to convey. Perhaps you want to show that you are a smiley, bubbly person, or a shy, observant person. You might create an image that looks artsy, athletic, or fashion-forward.

Draw the avatar you picture in your head.

In the metaverse, people can do things that are impossible IRL. Remember that as you come up with the theme for your destination in the metaverse.

- **Brainstorm.** Take a moment to think about your favorite video games and digital environments. What styles are eye-catching? When you are exploring a digital environment, what do you find most interesting? What actions, goals, and quests are the most fun?
    - First, write down the things you like about the other games and platforms you enjoy.
    - Then let your imagination soar. List all the amazing things you can think of for your avatar to do in an online world. What kind of space do you want to create? Somewhere magical? Somewhere futuristic? Do you want characters to play around in nature, or inside a building?

- **Design interactive spaces.** Think of your digital universe as a series of settings that can be added together to build a whole world.
  - Start by designing one room first. Picture the walls and the floor. Imagine where the doors and windows go. Think of all the furniture and objects that might fill up your space.
  - Below are just a few ideas of what you might put in your room. Use them as inspiration, or use tracing paper to create a template and trace the furniture you want to place in your space.

- What other spaces might you design? A room inside a castle, a spaceship, or your dream house? Or perhaps you want to create an outdoor space, complete with trees and a pond. Draw more settings and see how they connect.

- **Color your world.** What colors will you use to bring your world to life? From bright neon shades to dark, moody hues, the options are endless. Choose a color scheme and color in your drawings.

- **Engage your senses.** Now that you know what your world looks like, take a minute to think about what it sounds like. Do you hear birds chirping, kids laughing, or roller coasters whooshing by? Is there music playing in the background? If so, what kind? Upbeat and full of bass, or more mellow and jazzy? With your immense imagination, you are sure to choose the right sounds for your landscape.

- **Name your creation.** What will you call your new digital world? Name the place you have invented. Then create a logo for your digital world. For the logo, you might show the full name of your world or an acronym for the name. An acronym is a word made up of the first initials of each word in a term or phrase. Make sure the colors of your logo match the colors you use in your world. Find clever ways to decorate the logo that hint at the vibes or goals of the world.

Celebrate your creativity by sharing your ideas, drawings, and logo with your family, teachers, or friends!

WHAT'S YOUR ROLE IN THE METAVERSE?

Answer these questions to see which job might be right for you.

1. What do you like to do in your free time?
   A. Play video games
   B. Listen to music
   C. Write or act out stories
   D. Draw, paint, or doodle

2. Your birthday is coming up. Which present would you love to get?
   A. A robot I can program myself
   B. A great pair of headphones
   C. Tickets to a local theater performance
   D. Art supplies

3. You are volunteering at a fundraiser for your school. Which task do you take on?
   A. Setting up a donation and ticket-buying website
   B. Making a playlist that would keep everyone energized
   C. Helping pick the theme. (Fashion show or field day?)
   D. Designing the posters and tickets for the event

4. When you are watching movies, what do you think about?
   A. How do they make those special effects? Can I do that?
   B. I love how the music can stir my emotions. It can make me nervous—or make me cry!
   C. What is going to happen next? How can the main character get out of this situation?
   D. I notice the costumes and the cinematography.

5. You have a family gathering coming up. What group activity would you love to lead?

    A. Flying drones to take photos and videos of the group

    B. Karaoke!

    C. Playing charades

    D. Tie-dying shirts

ANSWER KEY

Look at your answers. Which letter did you choose most often?

Mostly As
Software Engineer

You're not afraid to dive into computer science and explore what your coding skills can do. Vibrant online worlds cannot come to life without coders and engineers—and you could be one of them!

Mostly Bs
Sound Designer

You've got an ear for audio. Whether making melodies or matching sound effects to motion, you would have a blast engaging people's senses while they explore digital spaces.

Mostly Cs
World Builder

Video games and online universes need storywriters to devise the rules, options, goals, and possibilities for every space. And you've got the imagination and storytelling chops to do just that.

Mostly Ds
Visual Artist

Drawing, doodling, painting, crafting, sculpting . . . You are always happiest when you let your creative juices flow freely. One day, your designs could live in the metaverse. Your art knows no limits!

GLOSSARY

3D artist (noun) — a person who uses computer software to create three-dimensional images, such as characters, props, and environments

animator (noun) — a person who creates images and makes them appear to move

audio engineering (noun) — a field that deals with the technical aspects of recording and working with sound

audio producer (noun) — a person who manages the recording process for a song, podcast, video game, online experience, or other piece of content

content design (noun) — a field in which people use words to help make products easier to understand and use

game producer (noun) — a person who oversees the creation of video games, often by managing the budget, the schedule, and the team making the game

marketer (noun) — a person who promotes or sells a product or service

mobility (noun) — the ability to move around easily

product designer (noun) — a person who creates digital experiences or services that are useful and engaging for people

product lead (noun) — a person who monitors the development of new services or experiences through all stages (from the idea stage through design, testing, and launch)

prototype (noun) — a model or early sample of a product

Silicon Valley (noun) — a region in Northern California that is home to many of the world's largest computer and technology companies

software architect (noun) — a computer programmer who makes decisions on how a system works and sets rules for other programmers to follow

startup (noun) — a newly formed business

virtual reality (noun) — a computer-generated 3D environment that, when viewed through a screen in a headset or glasses, gives the user the feeling that they are actually there

VR headset (noun) — a device worn over the eyes that allows the user to explore 3D computer-generated worlds and experiences

ABOUT META

Meta builds technologies that help people connect, find communities, and grow businesses. When Facebook launched in 2004, it changed the way people connect. Apps like Messenger, Instagram, and WhatsApp further empowered billions around the world. Now Meta is moving beyond 2D screens toward immersive experiences like augmented and virtual reality to help build the next evolution in social technology.

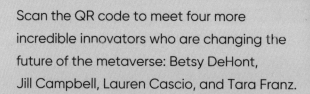

Scan the QR code to meet four more incredible innovators who are changing the future of the metaverse: Betsy DeHont, Jill Campbell, Lauren Cascio, and Tara Franz.

THE ILLUSTRATORS

Rebel Girls works with extraordinary female artists from all over the world. Here are the talented women who created portraits for this book:

ESTHER LALANNE, **FRANCE**, 29, 41
HANNAH AGOSTA, **US**, 15, 23, 39
JIAWEN CHEN, **CHINA**, 13, 33
NOA DENMON, **US**, cover, 9, 21
SALINI PERERA, **CANADA**, 7, 37
SOFIE BIRKIN, **UK**, 17, 27, 31
THUMY PHAN, **VIETNAM**, cover, 11, 19
XMX.LUO, **UK**, cover, 25, 35

Listen to more empowering stories on the Rebel Girls app!

Download the app to listen to beloved Rebel Girls stories. Filled with the adventures and accomplishments of women and girls from around the world and throughout history, the Rebel Girls app is designed to entertain, inspire, and build confidence in listeners everywhere.

MORE BOOKS!

For more stories about amazing women and girls, check out other Rebel Girls books.

QUESTIONS for REBEL GIRLS

How would you react?
What would you do?
Who do you want to be?

QUIZZES for REBEL GIRLS

Explore your personality, strengths, style, and more!

REBEL GIRLS LEAD

25 TALES OF POWERFUL WOMEN

REBEL GIRLS CHAMPIONS

25 TALES OF UNSTOPPABLE ATHLETES

REBEL GIRLS POWERFUL PAIRS

25 TALES OF MOTHERS AND DAUGHTERS

REBEL GIRLS CLIMATE WARRIORS

25 TALES OF WOMEN WHO PROTECT THE EARTH

REBEL GIRLS AWESOME ENTREPRENEURS

25 TALES OF WOMEN BUILDING BUSINESSES

REBEL GIRLS ANIMAL ALLIES

25 TALES OF WOMEN WORKING WITH WILDLIFE

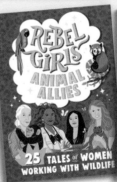

REBEL GIRLS CELEBRATE NEURODIVERSITY

25 TALES OF CREATIVE THINKERS

REBEL GIRLS ROCK

25 TALES OF WOMEN IN MUSIC

REBEL GIRLS CELEBRATE PRIDE

25 TALES OF SELF-LOVE AND COMMUNITY

REBEL GIRLS LEVEL UP

25 TALES OF WOMEN IN GAMING AND TECH

REBEL GIRLS DADS AND DAUGHTERS

25 TALES OF TEAMWORK AND FUN

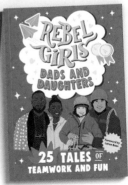

ABOUT REBEL GIRLS

Rebel Girls, a certified B Corporation, is a global, multi-platform empowerment brand dedicated to helping raise the most inspired and confident generation of girls through content, experiences, products, and community. Originating from an international best-selling children's book, Rebel Girls amplifies stories of real-life, extraordinary women throughout history, geography, and field of excellence. With a growing community of 30 million self-identified Rebel Girls spanning more than 100 countries, the brand engages with Generation Alpha through its book series, premier app and audio content, events, and merchandise. To date, Rebel Girls has sold more than 11 million books in 50 languages and reached 40 million audio listens. Award recognition includes the *New York Times* bestseller list, the 2022 Apple Design Award for Social Impact, multiple Webby Awards for family & kids and education, and Common Sense Media Selection honors, among others.

As a B Corp, we're part of a global community of businesses that meet high standards of social and environmental impact.

Join the Rebel Girls Community!
Visit rebelgirls.com and join our email list for exclusive sneak peeks, promos, activities, and more. You can also email us at hello@rebelgirls.com.

    YouTube: youtube.com/RebelGirls
    App: rebelgirls.com/audio
    Podcast: rebelgirls.com/podcast
    Facebook: facebook.com/rebelgirls
    Instagram: @rebelgirls
    Email: hello@rebelgirls.com
    Web: rebelgirls.com

If you liked this book, please take a moment to review it wherever you prefer!